STORIES

From My Life

JAMES E. FAUST

DESERET
BOOK

Library of Congress Catalog-in-Publication Data

Faust, James E., 1920-
    Stories from my life / James E. Faust.
        p. cm.
    Includes bibliographical references and index.
    ISBN 1-57345-968-2 (alk. paper)
    1. Christian life—Mormon authors. 2. Faust, James E., 1920.
I. Title.
BX8656 .F379 2001
289.3'092—dc21   2001000223

Printed in the United States of America   72082-6821
10   9   8   7   6   5   4   3   2   1

CONTENTS

PREFACE

Throughout my life, I have been blessed with countless experiences that, on reflection, have helped me to better understand the Lord's plan for His children, as well as my need to live a life that is in complete harmony with His teachings. In many cases, these experiences have been my own, while at other times I have benefited greatly from observing the faith and strength of others.

In the many talks I have given over the years, I have, as it seemed appropriate, shared a number of these stories to help illustrate various principles of the gospel. It is in that same spirit that some of these stories have been collected in this volume—that the reader's faith, understanding, and commitment might be strengthened, in the same way mine has been throughout my life.

James E. Faust
January 2001

1

A CRITICAL CROSSROAD

*Honesty is a principle, and we have our moral agency
to determine how we will apply this principle. We
have the agency to make choices; but ultimately, we
will be accountable for each choice we make. We
may deceive others, but there is One we will never
deceive.*

In the fateful war year of 1942, I was inducted into the
United States Army Air Corps. One cold night at Cha-
nute Field, Illinois, I was given all-night guard duty. As I
walked around my post, I meditated and pondered the whole
miserable long night through. By morning I had come to
some firm conclusions. I was engaged to be married and knew
that I could not support a wife on a private's pay. In a day or
two, I filed my application for officer's candidate school.

Shortly thereafter, I was summoned before the Board of Inquiry.

The questions asked of me at the officers' Board of Inquiry took a very surprising turn. Nearly all of them centered upon my missionary service and beliefs. "Do you smoke?" "Do you drink?" "What do you think of others who smoke and drink?" I had no trouble answering these questions.

"Do you pray?" "Do you believe that an officer should pray?" The officer asking these last questions was a hard-bitten career soldier. He did not look like he had prayed very often. I pondered. Would I give him offense if I answered how I truly believed? I wanted to be an officer very much so that I would not have to do all-night guard duty and KP, but mostly so my sweetheart and I could afford to be married.

I decided not to equivocate and responded that I did pray and that I felt officers might seek divine guidance as some truly great generals had done. I added that I thought that officers should be prepared to lead their men in all appropriate activities, if the occasion requires, including prayer.

More interesting questions came. "In times of war should not the moral code be relaxed? Does not the stress of battle justify men in doing things that they would not do when at home under normal situations?"

I recognized that here was a chance perhaps to make some points and look broad-minded. I knew perfectly well that the men who were asking me this question did not live by the standards that I had been taught. The thought flashed through my mind that perhaps I could say that I had my own beliefs but did not wish to impose them on others. But there seemed to flash before my mind the faces of the many people to whom I had taught the law of chastity as a missionary. In the end I simply said, "I do not believe there is a double standard of morality."

I left the hearing resigned to the fact that these hard-bitten officers would not like the answers I had given to their questions and would surely score me very low. A few days later when the scores were posted, to my astonishment I had passed. I was in the first group taken for officer's candidate school! I graduated, became a second lieutenant, married my sweetheart, and we "lived together happily ever after."

This was one of the critical crossroads of my life. Not all of the experiences in my life turned out the way I wanted them to, but they have always strengthened my faith.

2

THE BEST STAND OF HAY

The payment of tithing seems to facilitate keeping the spiritual battery charged in order to make it through the times when the spiritual generator has been idle or not working.

As a boy I learned a great lesson of faith and sacrifice as I worked on my grandfather's farm during the terrible economic depression of the 1930s. The taxes on the farm were delinquent, and Grandfather, like so many, had no money. There was a drought in the land, and some cows and horses were dying for lack of grass and hay. One day when we were harvesting what little hay there was in the field, Grandfather told us to take the wagon to the corner of the field where the best stand of hay stood and fill the wagon as full as we could and take it to the tithing yard as payment of his tithing in kind.

I wondered how Grandfather could use the hay to pay tithing when some of the cows that we were depending upon to sustain us might starve. I even questioned if the Lord expected that much sacrifice from him. Ultimately, I marveled at his great faith that somehow the Lord would provide. The legacy of faith he passed on to his posterity was far greater than money because he established in the minds of his children and grandchildren that above all he loved the Lord and His holy work over other earthly things. He never became wealthy, but he died at peace with the Lord and with himself.

I was taught more about the spirit of tithing by President Henry D. Moyle, who lived in my ward when I was serving as a young bishop. One tithing settlement, President Moyle, who at this time was a member of the Council of the Twelve, came in and declared, "Bishop, this is a full tithe and a little bit more, because that's the way we have been blessed."

Sister Yaeko Seki tells of coming to understand this same great truth in these words: "My family and I were spending a day at the Japan Alps National Park. . . . I was pregnant with our fourth child and was feeling rather tired, so I lay down under the trees. . . . I began thinking about our financial problems. My heart became overwhelmed, and I burst into tears. 'Lord, we are full-tithe payers. We have sacrificed so much. When will the windows of heaven open unto us and our burdens be lightened?'

"I prayed with all my heart. Then I turned to watch my husband and children playing and laughing together. . . . Suddenly, the Spirit testified to me that my blessings were abundant and that my family was the greatest blessing Heavenly Father could give me" (Yaeko Seki, "The Windows of Heaven," *Tambuli*, March 1992, 17).

3

It May Not Seem to Hurt as Much

In the many trials in life, when . . . weaknesses make
us less than we should ever be, there can come the
healing salve of the unreserved love in the grace of
God.

One summer our family, with several other families, went on an outing near Wanship, Utah. We camped in tents along the wooded banks of a beautiful river that flowed through Kamas Valley.

My friends and I spent many happy, carefree hours walking though the meadows or hunting varmints. These animals were considered pests because they ate the tender shoots the livestockmen needed for their sheep to graze on.

One afternoon while we were out hunting, I was accidentally shot at close range just above my knee. When the

.22 caliber slug passed through my leg, it felt like a hot poker was going into my flesh. As the blood ran down my leg, it became numb. My hunting companions helped me to our tent a short distance away, and I called to my father to show him what had happened. He and the other men bandaged my leg to control the bleeding. They helped me into our family car, and Father drove me to Coalville, Utah, where the near-est doctor lived.

When we reached the doctor's office, he laid me on an examining table. He looked at my bullet wound carefully, and then explained that it must be sterilized.

When I understood how the wound was to be sterilized, I was afraid of the pain I might have and also that I would cry. I didn't want to cry. I wanted to show my father how brave I could be. In my heart, I said a silent prayer that Heavenly Father would help me so that no matter how bad it hurt I wouldn't cry.

The doctor took a rod, about the size used to clean a gun barrel, and threaded a piece of sterilized gauze through a hole in one end like a giant needle. As my father held my hand, I gritted my teeth, shut my eyes, and tried to hold still while the doctor took the rod and pushed it through the hole in my leg. When it came out the other side, he changed the gauze, put fresh antiseptic on it, and pulled it back through the hole. He pushed it back and forth three times.

Heavenly Father heard my silent prayer, for the operation

did not seem to hurt as much as I thought it would. I didn't cry!

Since then, as problems and difficulties have come into my life, I have tried to face them by relying more on the help of our Heavenly Father than on the comfort that comes from tears. I learned the valuable lesson that the pain of life's problems doesn't seem to be so great if I don't cry about them.

4

DELIVERING IN OUR DEALINGS

Unfairness and injustice result principally from one person seeking an advantage or an edge over another. Those who follow such a practice demean themselves greatly.

During World War II, I came home on leave early one September. It was time to put peaches in bottles to preserve them for winter. My beloved mother-in-law called an old friend, George B. Andrus, of Holladay in the Salt Lake valley. The conversation on the telephone was brief: "George, do you have any peaches for sale?" Mother asked.

Patriarch Andrus answered, "I have a few, but they are not very good." I volunteered to drive Mother Wright to pick up the peaches. When we arrived she said, "George, where are your peaches?"

Brother Andrus opened his garage door, and I saw bushel baskets filled with large golden fruit with red kisses from sun ripening. Each basket was filled so full that when I lifted them into the trunk of the car some of the luscious peaches on top of the piled basket rolled off and bruised. Brother Andrus immediately replaced them with other perfect fruit.

On the way home I said to Mother Wright, "What did he mean when he said his fruit was not very good?"

She answered, "If you knew George Andrus, you would know that any fruit he would put on the market would be good and that he would give more than full value."

I wondered what the fruit would have been like if George had said it was good. Brother Andrus's self-imposed expectations led him to go beyond what we expected of him in his dealings with us.

5

"SUFFER THE LITTLE CHILDREN"

I am grateful for people on the earth who love and appreciate little children.

Some years ago, I found myself late at night on an airplane bulging with passengers going north from Mexico City to Culiacan. The seats in the plane were close together, and every seat was taken, mostly by the gracious people of Mexico. Everywhere inside the plane there were packages and carry-on luggage of all sizes.

A young woman came down the aisle with four small children, the oldest of which appeared to be about four and the youngest a newborn. She was also trying to manage a diaper bag and a stroller and some bags. The children were tired, crying, and fussing. As she found her seat in the airplane, the passengers around her, both men and women, literally sprang to her aid. Soon the children were being lovingly and tenderly comforted and cared for by the passengers. They were passed from one passenger to another all over the airplane.

The result was an airplane full of baby-sitters. The children settled down in the caring arms of those who cradled them and, before long, went to sleep. Most remarkable was that a few men who were obviously fathers and grandfathers tenderly cradled and caressed the newborn child without any false, macho pride. The mother was freed from the care of her children most of the flight.

The only thing I felt bad about was that no one passed the baby to me! I relearned that appreciation for little children, and thoughtfulness and kindness to them, are an expression of the Savior's love for them.

6

OUR DEBT OF GRATITUDE

The motivation for our pioneer forebears came from a
true conversion in the center of their souls.

How can we pay our debt of gratitude for the heritage of faith demonstrated by pioneers in many lands across the earth who struggled and sacrificed so that the gospel might take root? How is thankfulness expressed for the intrepid handcart pioneers who, by their own brute strength, pulled their meager belongings in handcarts across the scorching plains and through the snows of the high mountain passes to escape persecution and find peaceful worship in these valleys? How can the debt of gratitude possibly be paid by the descendants of the Martin and the Willie and the other handcart companies for the faith of their forebears?

One of these intrepid souls was Emma Batchelor, a young

English girl traveling without family. She started out with the Willie Handcart Company, but by the time they reached Fort Laramie, they were ordered to lighten their loads. Emma was directed to leave the copper kettle in which she carried all of her belongings.

She refused to do this and set it by the side of the road and sat down on it. She knew that the Martin company was only a few days behind. She had been privileged to start with the Willie company, and when the Martin company caught up, she joined the Paul Gourley family.

A young son wrote many years later: "Here we were joined by Sister Emma Batchelor. We were glad to have her because she was young and strong and meant more flour for our mess." It was here that Sister Gourley gave birth to a child, and Emma acted as the midwife and loaded the mother and the child in the cart for two days, which Emma helped pull.

Those who died in the Martin company were mercifully relieved of the suffering of others with frozen feet, ears, noses, or fingers—which maimed them for the rest of their lives. Emma, age twenty-one, however, was a fortunate one. She came through the ordeal whole.

A year later, she met Brigham Young, who was surprised that she was not maimed, and she told him, "Brother Brigham, I had no one to care for me or to look out for me, so I decided I must look out for myself. I was the one who called out when Brother Savage warned us [not to go]. I was at fault in that, but I tried to make up for it. I pulled my share at the cart every day. When we came to a stream, I stopped and took off my shoes and stockings and outer skirt and put them on top of the cart. Then, after I got the cart across, I came back and carried little Paul over on my back. Then I sat down and scrubbed my feet hard with my woolen neckerchief and put on dry shoes and stockings."

The descendants of these pioneers can partially settle the account by being true to the cause for which their ancestors suffered so much to be part of.

7

SETTING A STANDARD

We have all seen men who think they are not account-
able to the laws of men or of God. They seem to feel
that the rules of human conduct do not apply to them.

A friend related this experience her husband had while attending medical school. "Getting into medi- cal school is pretty competitive, and the desire to do well and be successful puts a great deal of pressure on the new incoming freshmen. My husband had worked hard on his studies and went to attend his first examination. The honor system was expected behavior at the medical school. The professor passed out the examination and left the room. Within a short time, students started to pull little cheat papers out from under their papers or from their pockets. My husband recalled his heart beginning to pound as he realized it is pretty hard to compete against cheaters. About that time, a tall, lanky student stood up in the back of the room and stated: 'I left my hometown and put my wife and three little babies in an upstairs apartment and worked very hard to get into medical school. And I'll turn in the first one of you who cheats, and *you better believe it!*' They believed it. There were many sheepish expressions, and those cheat papers started to disappear as fast as they had appeared. He set a standard for the class, which eventually graduated the largest group in the school's history." (This story is given as related by Janette Hales Beckham.)

The young, lanky medical student who challenged the cheaters was J. Ballard Washburn, who became a respected physician and in later years received special recognition from the Utah Medical Association for his outstanding service as a medical doctor. He also served as a General Authority and then as the president of the Las Vegas Temple.

8

WITHSTANDING THE THORNS OF LIFE

Regardless of the saturation of wickedness around us,
we must stay free from the evil of the world.

It seems that no matter how carefully we walk through life's paths, we pick up some thorns, briars, and slivers. As a young boy, when school was out for the summer and we went to the farm, off came our shoes. The shoes stayed off all summer long, except for special occasions. For the first week or two, when our feet were tender, the smoothest pebble or stick would be painful. But as the weeks came and went, the soles of our feet toughened so that they could withstand almost anything in the path except thistles, of which there seemed to be more than any other weed.

And so it is with life: as we grow and mature and keep close to Him who was crowned with thorns, our souls seem to get stronger in withstanding the challenges, our resolve hardens, our wills become firmer, and our self-discipline increases to protect us from the evils of this world. These evils are so omnipresent, however, that we must always walk in the paths which are the most free of the thistles of earthly temptation.

9

THE GOOD THAT CAN GROW
OUT OF TRAGEDY

In the pain, the agony, and heroic endeavors of life,
we pass through a refiner's fire, and the insignificant
and the unimportant in our lives can melt away like
dross and make our faith bright, intact, and strong.

Jeff and Joyce Underwood, of Pocatello, Idaho, are friends
I have been grateful to come to know. They are parents of
Jeralee and their other five children. Jeff works on a building maintenance team that cares for some of our chapels in
Pocatello, Idaho. Joyce is a mother and homemaker. One day
in July 1993, their daughter Jeralee, age eleven, was going
door to door collecting money for her newspaper route. Jeralee never returned home—not that day, nor the next day, nor
the next, nor ever.

Two thousand people from the area had gone out day after day to search for her. Other churches sent support and food for the searchers. It was learned that Jeralee had been abducted and brutally murdered by an evil man. When her body was found, the whole city was horrified and shocked. All segments of the community reached out to Joyce and Jeff in love and sympathy. Some became angry and wanted to take vengeance.

After Jeralee's body was found, Jeff and Joyce appeared with great composure before the television cameras and other media to publicly express their profound thanks to all who had helped in the search and who had extended sympathy and love. Joyce said, "I know our Heavenly Father has heard and answered our prayers, and he has brought our daughter back to us." Jeff said, "We no longer have doubt about where she is." Joyce continued, "I have learned a lot about love this week, and I also know there is a lot of hate. I have looked at the love and want to feel that love, and not the hate. We can forgive."

Elder Joe J. Christensen and I, representing the General Authorities, were among the thousands privileged to attend Jeralee's funeral service. The Holy Spirit blessed that gathering in a remarkable way and spoke peace to the souls of those who attended. Later, President Kert W. Howard, Jeralee's stake president, wrote, "The Underwoods have received letters from people both in and out of the Church stating that they prayed for Jeralee, and they hadn't prayed in years, and because of this, they had a renewed desire to return to the Church." President Howard continued, "We will never know the extent of activation and rededication this single event has caused. Who knows the far-reaching effects Jeralee's life will have for generations untold?" Many have come into the Church because they wanted to know what kind of a religion could give the Underwoods their spiritual strength.

I mention the good coming from this tragic event with Jeralee's parents' full approval and encouragement. Their sweet daughter was like the lad who had only five barley loaves and two small fishes to give to the cause of the Savior, but by the power of God, countless thousands have been spiritually fed.

10

NURTURING A SIMPLE FAITH

An untroubled faith can come by prayer, study, and a submissive willingness to keep as many command-ments as we can.

Several years ago, Elder and Sister F. Arthur Kay and I visited the beautiful and exotic island of Tahiti. Our flight arrived at the Papeete airport at about four in the morning. We were met at the airport by a group of local Church leaders headed by Regional Representative Victor Cave. We quickly assembled our bags and headed for the hotel to get what rest we could before the day's activities began. Our route took us through the deserted, dimly lighted streets of Papeete. In the dark, we saw the faint figure of a man crossing the street in front of Brother Cave's car. Brother Cave gave the man a lot of room to cross and told us, "That man is Brother So-and-so. He is hurrying to get to the temple. The first session of the temple doesn't begin until nine o'clock, but he wants to be there well in advance."

"How far away does he live?" asked Elder Kay. The answer: "Two or three blocks." Brother Cave indicated that the caretakers open the temple gates early and that this man comes in and watches the day begin within the sacred precincts of the beautiful temple in Papeete.

I marveled at the faith of that man, who is willing to forgo his sleep and other activities in order to meditate and contemplate. Some would no doubt say, "How foolish! How wasteful of time that could be spent sleeping or studying." I choose to hope that in those programmed hours of meditation and contemplation that faithful man is coming to know himself and his Creator.

It is important for us to nurture such a simple, untroubled faith. I urge complete acceptance of the absolutes of our own faith. At the same time, I urge you not to be unduly concerned about the intricacies, the complexities, and any seeming contradictions that seem to trouble many of us. Sometimes we spend time satisfying our intellectual egos and trying to find all the answers before we accept any.

11

BEARING OUR RESPONSIBILITIES

*If we look upon fulfilling of assignments as building
the kingdom of God and as being an opportunity as
well as a privilege and an honor, then assignments
and challenges should certainly be given to every able
member.*

E ver since I was first in Egypt in World War II, I have
been interested in ancient ruins. There is a fascination
in observing why some columns still stand and others
have toppled over. Very frequently those still standing do so
because they bear a weight on top. There is, I believe, a par-
allel principle in leadership. Those who stand faithful to their
priesthood are often those who bear some weight of responsibility. Those involved are those most likely to be committed.
So a successful quorum leader will want all of those in his

quorum to have an opportunity to serve with some kind of calling appropriate to the circumstances.

One Sunday morning I sat in an elders quorum meeting. The members of the presidency were fine, capable young men; but when they got around to sharing the quorum responsibilities and getting the work done, they limited it to those who were present and who would volunteer. Not one assignment was given.

One of the first principles we must keep in mind is that the work of the Lord goes forward through assignments. Leaders receive and give assignments. This is an important part of the necessary principle of delegating. No one appreciates a willing volunteer more than I, but the total work cannot be done as the Lord wants it done merely by those doing the work who may be present at meetings. I have often wondered what the earth would look like if the Lord in the Creation had left the work to be done only by volunteers.

12

THE VERY APPEARANCE
OF EVIL

We cannot be passive; we must actively avoid evil.

At the time I was finishing law school, I was called by Elder Harold B. Lee to serve as a counselor in our ward's bishopric. During the interview, Elder Lee asked me if Ruth and I had playing cards in our home. I said, "Yes, we do," and explained that my former missionary companions and I got together socially and played the game of Hearts. He didn't tell me to get rid of the cards. What he said was, "From this day forward, you must not only avoid evil, you must avoid the very appearance of evil."

I don't know that I've always done that, but I've tried. And I do try. But I learned from that interview that it is incumbent upon all of us—as leaders and as members of the

Church—to not do anything in our personal conduct that would give anybody else license to do something they have seen us do.

13

A LESSON IN LEADERSHIP

*Those who are called to lead in the ministry of the
Master are not called to be chiefs or dictators. They
are called to be good shepherds.*

Some years ago I was traveling in the Rosario Argentina
Mission up in the northern part of Argentina. As we
were traveling along the road, we passed a large herd
of cattle being moved. The herd was moving peaceably and
without difficulty. The herd was quiet. There were no dogs.
Out in front leading the herd were three gauchos on horse-
back, each about fifteen or twenty yards apart. These three
horsemen were slumped forward in their saddles, completely
relaxed, confident that the herd would follow them. At the
rear of the herd was a single rider bringing up the rear. He,
too, was slumped forward in his saddle as if he were sleeping.

The whole herd moved peacefully, quietly, and was subdued. From that experience it seemed obvious to me that leadership is about three-fourths show-the-way and about one-fourth follow-up.

14

EARNING THE CONFIDENCE
OF OTHERS

True disciples are those who go beyond simply believing. They act out their beliefs.

W hile I was serving as Area Supervisor in South America many years ago, a most unforgettable experience happened in Montevideo, Uruguay. I wanted to change some money because I was living in Brazil at the time, so Brother Carlos Pratt took me to a money exchange house in downtown Montevideo. He introduced me to one of the officials, and the official said they would change $1,000. I did not have $1,000 in cash and had only a check drawn on a bank in Salt Lake City. The exchange house had never done business with me before. In fact, they had never seen me before and could not expect to ever see me again. They had no way to verify if I had $1,000 on deposit in the bank upon which I had drawn the check. But they accepted my check without hesitation—based solely on the fact that I was a Mormon and that they had previously done business with other Mormons. Frankly, I was both grateful and pleased because of their confidence.

15

Making It Do, or Doing Without

To be industrious involves energetically managing our circumstances to our advantage.

Brother Joseph Stucki, a faithful Church member, died Christmas Eve in 1927 after a short illness, leaving his wife with seven children, the eldest son being on a mission. Two of the children and a nephew she was rearing were later taken in death. Another son was also sent on a mission. This was accomplished by much hard work—taking in sewing and living on a few dollars per month from an insurance policy.

During this difficult time, flour was being distributed to needy members of the ward. Some of the young men had been asked to deliver it. A bag of flour was brought to Sister Stucki's home. Since she felt that there were other families in the ward that needed that flour worse than she did, she declined to keep it, telling the young man that she was trying to teach her family to be independent and self-reliant. While worthy members of the Church should feel free to accept help from the Church proffered by the bishop, Sister Stucki was trying to teach the young man who came to her door a lesson. You see, the young man delivering the flour was her own son! All the surviving children attended college and became very successful people. They lived by the motto, "Make it do, or do without."

16

AN EARNED LEGACY

The importance of the Book of Mormon in our history and theology cannot be overestimated. The Book of Mormon is the text for this dispensation.

Some time ago I held in my hand my mother's copy of her favorite book. It was a timeworn copy of the Book of Mormon. Almost every page was marked; in spite of tender handling, some of the leaves were dog-eared, and the cover was worn thin. No one had to tell her that one can get closer to God by reading the Book of Mormon than by any other book. She was already there. She had read it, studied it, prayed over it, and taught from it. As a young man I held her book in my hands and tried to see, through her eyes, the great truths of the Book of Mormon to which she so readily testified and which she so greatly loved.

As a young boy in the Cottonwood Ward, I was greatly impressed when I listened to James H. Moyle tell in sacrament meeting of his having heard both Martin Harris and David Whitmer, two of the witnesses of the Book of Mormon, affirm their testimony concerning that book. They, along with Oliver Cowdery, had testified in connection with the original publication of the Book of Mormon "that an angel of God came down from heaven, and he brought and laid before our eyes, that we beheld and saw the plates, and the engravings thereon; and we . . . bear record that these things are true" ("The Testimony of Three Witnesses," Book of Mormon).

When James H. Moyle visited David Whitmer, Brother Whitmer was an old man; he was out of the Church and was living in a log cabin in Richmond, Missouri. Of this visit to David Whitmer, James H. Moyle stated in an address on March 22, 1908: "I went to his humble home, . . . and I told him . . . as a young man starting out in life I wanted to know from him . . . what he knew about the Book of Mormon, and what about the testimony he had published to the world concerning it. He told me in all the solemnity of his advanced years, that the testimony he had given to the world, and which was published in the Book of Mormon, was true, every word of it, and that he had never deviated nor departed in any particular from that testimony, and that nothing in the world could separate him from the sacred message that was delivered to him. I still wondered if it was not possible that he could have been deceived, . . . so I induced him to relate to me, under such cross-examination as I was able to interpose, every detail of what took place. He described minutely the spot in the woods, the large log that separated him from the angel, and that he saw the plates from which the Book of Mormon was translated, that he handled them, and that he did hear the voice of God declare that the plates were correctly translated. I asked him if there was any possibility for him to have been deceived, and that it was all a mistake, but he said, 'No'" (quoted in Gordon B. Hinckley, *James Henry Moyle*, Salt Lake City: Deseret Book, 1951, 366–67).

However, the Book of Mormon did not yield its profound message to me as an unearned legacy. I question whether one can acquire an understanding of this great book except through singleness of mind and strong purpose of heart. We must ask not only if it is true, but also do it in the name of Jesus Christ. Said Moroni, "Ask God, the Eternal Father, in the name of Christ, if these things are not true; and if ye shall ask with a sincere heart, with real intent, having faith in Christ, he will manifest the truth of it unto you, by the power of the Holy Ghost" (Moroni 10:4).

I can now see more clearly through the eyes of my own understanding what my mother could see in her precious old worn-out copy of the Book of Mormon.

17

"What Can You Do?"

Learning and education have always been the hall-mark of the Latter-day Saints.

Many years ago I received an unwelcome but valuable message from my devoted father. After World War II was over, I was married and wanted to get on with my life. My memorable mission was finished before my military service. I was not anxious to become a student again and go back to the university where I had started some eight years before. My intended course would require another three years of intensive study, discipline, and poverty. With all of this in mind I said to my father, "I don't think I will go back to school. I'll just get a job or start a business and go forward in my life." Now, my father had completed law school after World War I as an older student with a wife and three children. His response was typically direct. He said bluntly, "What can you do?" His answer was so brutally honest that it hurt, but I could not ignore it. I went back to the university and completed the course. This frank but well-intentioned message changed my life.

18

STANDING ON HOLY GROUND

The gift of eternal life requires a willingness to sacrifice all we have and are in order to obtain it.

In 1992, as our family celebrated the 24th of July, we joined with the Saints of the Riverton Wyoming Stake. Under the direction of President Robert Lorimer and his counselors, the youth and youth leaders of that stake reenacted part of the handcart trek which took place in 1856. We started early in a four-wheel-drive van and went first to Independence Rock, where we picked up the Mormon Trail. We saw Devil's Gate a few miles up the road. Our souls were subdued when we arrived at the hallowed ground of Martin's Cove, the site where the Martin Handcart Company, freezing and starving, waited for the rescue wagons to come from

Salt Lake City. About fifty-six members of the Martin Handcart Company perished there from hunger and cold.

It was an emotional experience to see the Sweetwater River Crossing, where most of the five hundred members of the company were carried across the icy river by three brave young men. Later, all three of the boys died from the effects of the terrible strain and great exposure of that crossing. When President Brigham Young heard of this heroic act, he wept like a child, and later declared publicly: "That act alone will ensure C. Allen Huntington, George W. Grant and David P. Kimball an everlasting salvation in the Celestial Kingdom of God, worlds without end!" (Solomon F. Kimball, "Belated Emigrants of 1856," *Improvement Era,* Feb. 1914, 288).

We went farther along the trail to the site where the members of the Willie Handcart Company were rescued. We felt that we were standing on holy ground. At that site twenty-one members of that party died from starvation and cold. We continued to travel up over Rocky Ridge, seven thousand three hundred feet high. This is the highest spot on the Mormon Trail. The two-mile ascension to Rocky Ridge gains over seven hundred feet in altitude. It was very difficult for all of the pioneers to travel over Rocky Ridge. It was particularly agonizing for the members of the Willie Handcart Company, who struggled over the ridge in the fall of 1856 in a blizzard. Many had worn-out shoes, and the sharp rocks caused their feet to bleed, leaving a trail of blood in the snow.

As we walked over Rocky Ridge, two square nails and an old-style button were picked up. No doubt these objects were shaken loose going over the sharp rocks. My soul was sobered to be in that historic spot. Several of my ancestors crossed that ridge, though none were in the handcart companies. Not all of my forebears who started in the great exodus to the West made it even to Rocky Ridge. Two of them died at Winter Quarters.

As I walked over Rocky Ridge, I wondered if I have sacrificed enough. In my generation, I have not seen so much sacrifice by so many. I wonder what more I should have done, and should be doing, to further this work.

19

WILL WE ACCEPT THE GIFT?

We must constantly be reaching upward for the riches of eternity.

Many years ago I went to the hospital to give a blessing to a young man named Nick and his sister Michelle. Nick is a friend of mine and former home teaching companion, and his young life was threatened by diseased kidneys. Nick had not been well for a long time. Nick's older sister Michelle had offered to give him a precious gift to preserve his life: she offered one of her own kidneys.

The operation was successfully performed, but still in question was whether or not Nick's body would accept this priceless gift from Michelle. You see, Michelle had given the gift not knowing if it would be accepted. Fortunately it was accepted. In like manner, our Heavenly Father has given us so many wonderful gifts, regardless of whether they will be accepted. He has offered us his peace, his comfort, his love. All we have to do to accept his gifts is to be obedient and follow him.

20

A BLESSING FROM THE LORD

*A patriarchal blessing from an ordained patriarch can
give us a star to follow, which is a personal revelation
from God to each individual. If we follow this star,
we are less likely to stumble and be misled.*

I have heard Elder LeGrand Richards tell of a patriarch
who once said to a woman, "I have a wonderful blessing
for you." But when the patriarch laid his hands on the
head of the recipient, his mind went completely blank. He
apologized. "I was mistaken. I do not have a blessing for you.
It is the Lord who has the blessing for you." The woman came
back the next day and, after the patriarch had prayerfully
importuned the Lord, a blessing came that mentioned many
concerns known only to this good sister.

All blessings come from God. Our Heavenly Father

knows his children. He knows their strengths and weaknesses. He knows their capabilities and potential. Our patriarchal blessings indicate what He expects of us and what our potential can be.

Patriarchal blessings should be read humbly, prayerfully, and frequently. A patriarchal blessing is very sacred and personal but may be shared with close family members. It is a sacred guideline of counsel, promises, and information from the Lord; however, a person should not expect the blessing to detail all that will happen to him or her or to answer all questions. The fact that one's patriarchal blessing may not mention an important event in life, such as a mission or marriage, does not mean that it will not happen. In order to receive the fulfillment of our patriarchal blessings, we should treasure in our hearts the precious words they contain, ponder them, and so live that we will obtain the blessings in mortality and a crown of righteousness in the hereafter.

My own blessing is short, and it is limited to perhaps three-quarters of a page on one side, yet it has been completely adequate and perfect for me. I received my patriarchal blessing as I entered my early teenage years. The patriarch promised that my blessing would "be a comfort and a guide" to me throughout my life. As a boy I read it over and over again. I pondered each word. I prayed earnestly to understand fully the spiritual meaning. Having that blessing early in my life guided me through all of the significant events and challenges of my life. I did not fully understand the meaning of my blessing until I gained more maturity and experience. This blessing outlined some of the responsibilities I would have in the kingdom of God on earth.

President Heber J. Grant told of the patriarchal blessing he received: "That patriarch put his hands upon my head and bestowed upon me a little blessing that would perhaps be about one-third of a typewritten page. That blessing foretold my life to the present moment" (quoted in James R. Clark, comp., *Messages of the First Presidency of The Church of Jesus Christ of Latter-day Saints*, 6 vols., Salt Lake City: Bookcraft, 1965–75, 5:152).

21

FINDING THE SIGNAL POINT

I believe the Spirit of the Holy Ghost is the greatest
guarantor of inward peace in our unstable world.

My first radio was a crystal set. It was hard to tune to the frequency of a particular radio station. One had to literally scratch the receiving wire whisker over the top of the rough crystal to find the right pinpoint, a little valley or peak on the crystal, where the signal was received. Just a millimeter off on one side or the other of that point and you would lose the signal and get scratchy static. Over time, with patience and perseverance, good eyesight and a steady hand, you could learn to find the signal point on the crystal without too much difficulty.

So it is in learning to attune ourselves to the inspiration from God and tune out the scratchy static. We have to work at being tuned in. Most of us need a long time to become tuned in most of the time. When I was a young General Authority, President Marion G. Romney, who was in his seventies at the time, told us, "I know when I am working under the Spirit and when I am not." To be able to recognize when one is being guided by the Spirit is a supernal gift.

22

Spiritual Taproots

Some of us are naturally reserved and timid about bearing our testimony with words. Perhaps we should not be so timid.

Many years ago, we went to Manaus, Brazil, a city far upstream on the Amazon River, surrounded by jungle, to meet with the missionaries and the handful of Saints who were then in that area. We met in a very humble home with no glass panes in the windows. The weather was excessively hot. The children sat on the floor. The mission president, President Helio da Rocha Camargo, conducted the meeting and called on a faithful brother to give the opening prayer. The humble man responded, "I will be happy to pray, but may I also bear my testimony?" A sister was asked to lead the singing. She responded, "I would love to lead the singing, but please let me also bear my testimony."

And so it was all through the meeting with those who participated in any way. All felt impelled to bear their profound witness of the Savior and his mission and of the restoration of the gospel of Jesus Christ. All who were there reached deep down in their souls to their spiritual taproots, remembering the Savior's words that "where two or three are gathered together in my name, there am I in the midst of them" (Matthew 18:20).

This they did more as heirs to the kingdom of God than as Brazilian members of the Church.

23

POISE UNDER PRESSURE

For some, the refiner's fire causes a loss of belief and faith in God, but those with eternal perspective understand that such refining is part of the perfection process.

Some of the faculty at Brigham Young University, and many of the students, were present on February 7, 1993, in the Marriott Center for the nineteen-stake fireside and Church Education System broadcast. You will recall that when President Howard W. Hunter was at the pulpit, an intruder carrying a briefcase in one hand and something black in the other stepped on the stand and shouted, "Stop right there." He then ordered everybody but President Hunter to leave the stand. Many did leave, but President Hunter quietly and resolutely stayed at the pulpit. The assailant then demanded that President Hunter read aloud a prepared statement. President Hunter firmly declined to do so. The assailant picked the wrong man. I know of no man in this world who was more resolute, unflappable, and courageous than President Hunter. You will recall that when the assailant was momentarily distracted, he was pushed from the stand. President Hunter was lowered by the security guards and others to the floor for safety. After the incident, I am told that President Hunter's pulse was only seventy beats per minute!

You will recall that President Hunter collected himself and then began his prepared message saying, "Life has a fair number of challenges in it." Then his irrepressible sense of humor surfaced, and he added, "As demonstrated." He then went on with his message as though nothing had happened.

24

THE PERMANENCE OF
THE FAMILY

*We sometimes hear requests for a new program for
that group or a new organization for this group or a
new activity for the other group. We already have the
new program. It is called the family.*

Many years ago when I was a bishop, a conscientious
father came to me for counsel. He felt that the
many and frequent activities of the Church made
it difficult to have as much family togetherness as he and his
wife deemed necessary. The children had the idea that they
were not loyal to the Church if they did not participate fully
in every recreational activity. I told this caring father that
Church activities were to help him and his wife rear their
children. They as parents had not only the right but the duty

to determine the extent of their family's involvement in social activities. Family unity, solidarity, and harmony should be preserved. After all, a family is the permanent, basic unit of the Church.

25

THE WEIGHTIER MATTERS

Surely, repentance is one of the great principles of the gospel. No one is perfect, and we all have need to invoke this principle.

I fear that some of our greatest sins are sins of omission. These are some of the weightier matters of the law the Savior said we should not leave undone (Matthew 23:23). These are the thoughtful, caring deeds we fail to do, and feel so guilty for having neglected them.

As a small boy on the farm during the searing heat of the summer, I remember my grandmother, Mary Finlinson, cooking our delicious meals on a hot woodstove. When the wood box next to the stove became empty, Grandmother would silently pick up the box, go out to refill it from the pile of cedar wood outside, and bring the heavily laden box back into the house. I was so insensitive and so interested in the conversation in the kitchen, I sat there and let my beloved grandmother refill the kitchen wood box. I feel ashamed of myself and have regretted my omission for all of my life. I hope someday to ask for her forgiveness.

26

BEGIN WITH OUR OWN

If we feel we are relieved of our duty to our non-member neighbors because full-time missionaries happen to be working in our neighborhoods, it is most unfortunate.

When I was a boy, I remember attending the homecoming of Ames Bagley, who came home from a mission in a distant land across the sea. His mother, Sister Amanda Bagley, had been a wise stake Relief Society president. Sister Bagley was invited to speak at her son's homecoming sacrament meeting. In her response, she wondered why we send our missionaries so far, spend so much time, effort, and money to support missionaries far away when our next-door neighbors and friends at home have souls just as important and precious as those in distant lands. We may have a tendency to think if we are sending missionaries that we are taking care of our responsibilities for this important work. Yet all of us have neighbors, all of us have friends, and many of us have kinsmen who are not members.

Our interest in sharing the vision and blessings of the gospel should begin with our own. Andrew heard Christ speak and followed him and then, "He first findeth his own brother Simon, and saith unto him, We have found the Messias. . . . And he brought him to Jesus" (John 1:39–42). Lehi stated as he partook of the tree of life: "As I partook of the fruit, it filled my soul with exceeding great joy; wherefore, I began to be desirous that my family should partake of it also, for I knew that it was desirable above all other fruit" (1 Nephi 8:10–12).

27

WHAT IS OF WORTH

The dignity of self is greatly enhanced by looking up-
ward in the search for holiness.

When I was growing up in the Cottonwood area of Salt Lake County, it was the rural part of the valley. One of the men who had the greatest dignity and commanded the greatest respect was an old Scandinavian brother who, after walking a couple of miles, traveled by streetcar to work at the Salt Lake City Cemetery every day. His work was to water and mow the grass, tend the flowers, and dig the graves. He said little because he did not speak English well, but he was always where he should be, doing what he should do in a most dignified, exemplary way. He had no problems with ego, or with faith, for while he dug graves for a living, his work was to serve God. He was a man of little status, but of great worth.

Not far away from his humble home was where the more affluent people of our community lived. Many of the well-to-do were fine, honorable people; but some of them who had much status had little of real worth.

When the Savior called his disciples he was not looking for men and women of status, property, or fame. He was looking for those of worth and potential. They were an interesting group, those early disciples: the fishermen, the tax gatherer, and the others.

28

"On My Honor"

We have the agency to make choices; but, ultimately,
we will be accountable for each choice we make.

Honesty begins when we are young. When I was eleven years old, I looked forward eagerly to my magical twelfth birthday when I could become a deacon and a Scout. My mother helped me learn the Articles of Faith, the Scout Law and Motto, and other requirements so that I would have a good start when that special birthday arrived.

Since I had no sisters, my brothers and I were given some of the inside chores as well as outside ones, such as milking and taking care of the animals. One day Mother left me to wash the dishes and clean the kitchen while she attended to a sick neighbor. I agreed to do these duties but put off doing the dishes. Time ran out and they didn't get done. In fact, they didn't even get started. When Mother came home and saw the kitchen, she put on her apron and went to the sink. She spoke only three words, which stung worse than the sting of a dozen hornets. They were the first three words of the Scout Law: "On my honor." That day I resolved that I would never give my mother cause to repeat those words to me again.

29

A SPIRIT THAT SHONE

We do not seek a veneer painted on by a worldly brush but the pure, innate beauty that God has planted in our souls.

A few years ago I became acquainted with a delightful and wonderful new friend. He is charming, outgoing, and well-groomed. He is a successful businessman. His spirituality shines through his countenance. He was completely honest in our business relationship. After many contacts and several months, I noticed a slight limp in his walk which had not been obvious before. That led to a closer observation. It was surprising that when I looked past the gracious smile, I noticed that my friend was slightly hunchbacked, with a somewhat misshapen spine. These physical defects were so well hidden by natural goodness, warmth, and great charm that they were as nothing in the total man. My friend accepts his physical defects with humility and strength and completely compensates for them with his natural personality.

30

"A Fine Christian You Are"

Extending forgiveness, love, and understanding for
perceived shortcomings in our wives, husbands, chil-
dren, and associates makes it much easier to say,
"God, be merciful to me a sinner."

I was late in learning the value of the principle of praying
for those who despitefully use us. As a young lawyer, I was
handling a matter for the office forwarded by a lawyer
from Texas. The matter was successfully concluded, and the
settlement check came payable to the client and to our office
as joint payees to satisfy the attorneys' lien. As was the cus-
tom in our office, I endorsed the check and sent it down to
the corresponding attorney, having full confidence that he
would promptly remit the agreed-upon portion of the recovery. It did not come.

I wrote many letters. Months passed, and still there was no response. My associates were understanding, but it was not my money to forget or forgive. I felt I was being despitefully used. I thought about referring him to the Texas Bar Association for disciplinary action.

Then a thought hit me. I had not done what my mother had taught me as a child at her knee. I said to myself, "A fine Christian you are!" My conscience was pricked also because I was a bishop.

That night I got down on my knees and prayed earnestly for this person who I thought had despitefully used me.

Then, in the time that it takes for an airmail letter to come from Texas, a letter came with the explanation that this man had become very ill, had been in the hospital, had to close his office, and was ill for many months. He asked my forgiveness and advised that the check was enclosed.

31

A Christmas with No Presents

*The answer in the Christmas season and throughout
the year lies not in the receiving of earthly presents
and treasures, but in the forsaking of selfishness and
greed and in going forward, seeking and enjoying the
gifts of the Spirit.*

I have been thinking about what makes Christmas such a
great time in our lives. I am old enough to remember
many Christmases. They have all been glorious. But I
learned that it isn't just the presents that makes them great.
A Christmas without presents? No toys or dolls for children
to hold in their hands? Whoever heard of such a thing? I
remember such a Christmas with no presents.

When I was a young boy, our family was terribly poor.
Father had no job because he was going through law school

at the University of Utah. He had a wife and three young sons. Grandfather and Grandmother knew that we would have no Christmas if we did not come down to the farm in Millard County. So all of our family took the train from Salt Lake to Leamington, Utah. Where the money came from for the tickets, I will never know.

Grandfather and Uncle Esdras met us at the railroad crossing in Leamington with a team of big horses to pull the open sleigh through the deep snow to Oak City. It was so cold that the huge horses had icy chin whiskers and you could see their breath. I remember how old Jack Frost nipped my nose and the extreme cold made it hard to breathe. Grandmother had heated some rocks and put them in the bottom of the sleigh to help keep us warm. We were wrapped and tucked into some heavy camp quilts with just our noses sticking out. Accompanied by the tinkle of bells on leather straps on the harnesses of the horses, we musically traveled from Leamington over the ten miles to Oak City, where our beloved grandfather and grandmother lived. So many dear ones were there that we could hardly wait to arrive. When we got there it was warm and wonderful and exciting.

In the corner of the living room was the Christmas tree—a cedar cut from the hillside pasture. It was already partially decorated by Mother Nature with little berries that helped give it a strong smell. Our decorations were popcorn strings made by threading popcorn through a needle and a thread which had to be handled carefully or they would break and strew popcorn all over the floor.

We also had paper chains to put on the tree, made by cutting up old Sears and Montgomery Ward catalogs with the paper links pasted together with flour paste. The sticky flour paste got all over our hands, faces, and clothes. I wonder why they didn't put sugar in it! With cream it could also have been served for mush.

I do not remember any presents under the tree. I do remember that under the tree were popcorn balls made with strong, homemade molasses. When we bit into the popcorn balls, it felt like they were biting back!

On Christmas Eve we all gathered around the wood stove, enjoying the warm comfort of the fire and the pleasant aroma of the burning cedar wood. One of the uncles gave the opening prayer. We sang carols and hymns. One of our aunts read of the birth of Jesus and of the "good tidings of great joy" (Luke 2:10). "For unto you is born this day in the City of David a Saviour, which is Christ the Lord" (Luke 2:11). Grandfather and Grandmother then told us how much they loved us.

The next day was Christmas, and we had a glorious dinner. But before we ate, we all got down on our knees for family prayer. I was so hungry. Grandfather prayed for the longest time. You see, he had much to pray for. He prayed for moisture because there was a drought in the land and the crops had been meager. The fall grain had been planted in the dusty ground. What harvest there was could not be sold for much because of the low price caused by the great depression. The taxes on the farm were delinquent because there was no money to pay them. He also prayed for our large family, his cattle and horses, pigs and chickens, turkeys—he prayed over everything.

During Grandfather's long prayer, my youngest uncle became restless and gave me an irreverent pinch, hoping that I would shout to make things more exciting.

For dinner we had a huge tom turkey stuffed with delicious dressing. There was no celery in the dressing because we had only the ingredients that could be produced on the farm. But the dressing had plenty of bread, sage, sausage, and onions. There was an abundance of potatoes and gravy and pickles, beets, beans, and corn. Because Grandfather could trade wheat to the miller for flour, there was always fresh baked bread. To stretch the food, we were encouraged to take one bite of bread for every bite of other kinds of food. We had chokecherry jelly and ground-cherry jam. For dessert we had pumpkin and gooseberry pie. It was all delicious.

As I look back on that special Christmas now, the most memorable part was that we did not think about presents. There may have been some handmade mittens or a scarf given, but I do not recall any presents. Presents are wonderful, but I found that they are not essential to our happiness. I could not have been happier. There were no presents that could be seen and held and played with, but there were many wonderful gifts that could be felt.

There was the gift of boundless love. We knew God loved us. We all loved each other. We did not miss the presents because we had all these glorious gifts. It made me feel so wonderful and secure to belong and to be part of all that went on. We wanted nothing else. We did not miss the presents at all. I never remember a happier Christmas in my childhood.

With gifts such as these, I am sure everyone could feel as I did that wonderful Christmas so long ago when we had no presents to hold and play with. I would not have wanted to trade places with any prince of the world with his room full of toys. The gifts of love, peace, service, self, and faith so generously given made me feel fulfilled. It made me feel that I must be somebody special to be part of so much love. I wanted nothing else than more of these wonderful gifts that couldn't be handled or touched, but only felt.

32

THE DAY THE BISHOP SANG

*The Lord can do remarkable miracles with a person
of ordinary ability who is humble, faithful, and diligent in serving the Lord and who seeks to improve
himself or herself.*

An important dimension in learning to laugh at ourselves lies in not being afraid to make a mistake.
When I was a young bishop, we sought to have a
ward choir. We had a good choir leader, Brother Alex
Anderson. However, he encouraged the bishop to sing in the
choir. I felt that as a measure of support for Brother Anderson
and the others, I should try to sing with them, but things
went from bad to worse.

Brother Anderson liked to invite the choir members to
show off their talents by singing solos. One Sunday during

choir practice he asked that I sing a small solo. I found it very difficult to turn him down in front of the choir, so during sacrament meeting, when the choir sang I tried to sing the solo. I was so frightened that the paper trembled in my hand, and I could hardly hold it. I felt embarrassed and humiliated. All of my mask of dignity was gone.

After the meeting, as I walked down the aisle, I was met with warm smiles and expressions of understanding and support. Someone said, "Bishop, it surely makes us feel good to see you scared." That day the bishop became more human.

33

WELL-CHOSEN DREAMS

*In my opinion, the teaching, rearing, and training of
children requires more intelligence, intuitive understanding, humility, strength, wisdom, spirituality,
perseverance, and hard work than any other challenge
we might have in life.*

Zoroaster reminds us: "Nobody grows old merely by living a number of years. People grow old by deserting
their ideals. Years wrinkle the skin, but giving up
enthusiasm wrinkles the soul. Worry, doubt, self-distrust, fear,
and despair—these are the long years that bow the head and
turn the growing spirit back to dust. You are as young as your
faith and as old as your doubts; as young as your self-
confidence, as old as your fear; as young as your hope, as old
as your despair."

I hear some people say, "I am not important because I am not famous." Some years ago I was assigned by the Brethren to attend a stake conference in one of the most remote areas of Idaho. The stake president was a cattle rancher on a ranch high in the mountains. In this family was a mother who had thirteen children and had had thirteen natural miscarriages. We arrived at their home after our evening meeting. It was not luxurious, but comfortable and warm from the heat of a wood stove. I was given a bed on the front porch; a curtain was hung up on safety pins to give me some privacy. In the morning I got up and went to breakfast. A little boy, who has a different kind of spirit, came in, and the stake president said, "This is Johnny." A few minutes later we heard some-body sawing on the front door. The stake president, without raising his voice, simply said, "Johnny, come in." He came in and the evidence was in his hand—the saw. Apparently this was not an unusual occurrence. Then came little Mary. Mary had a harelip. And they brought a little baby in, maybe six months old. This great woman was rearing this family.

That morning we called on her in stake conference. She said, "We heard about Mary and nobody wanted her. We need a new truck, but when we saw her, we knew we needed her more than we needed the new truck. And then we heard about Johnny, who kind of listens to a different voice. I needed a new range in the kitchen, but when we met Johnny we knew we needed him more than we needed a new range in the kitchen. And I wanted a new love seat, but we heard about the baby, and we knew we needed the baby more than the love seat."

Then she went on to say, "The other evening I finished my work about midnight. My husband and all my children were asleep, and I was tired. I should have gone to bed, but I sat down in the rocker and thought about my childhood dreams. When I was a young girl I wanted to be rich and famous. And then I thought about all of my children asleep and my husband and how hard he has to work to be a good father to all of these children and a good spiritual father to all of the people in the stake. And I thought about how his calling as a stake president doesn't take away from the family—it adds to it."

She concluded, "I realized that I married the finest man in all the world. And as I counted my children, I realized then that I wouldn't trade places with my childhood dreams of being rich and famous."

34

THE POWER OF PRAYER

To control the great physical laws by the power of the priesthood, we need to understand and invoke the greater spiritual laws of faith, righteousness, and obedience.

For a number of years, I was privileged to work with the wonderful Saints in the islands of the sea. All my life I have seen the power of the priesthood used to heal and bless in many ways. But I have seen the Polynesian Saints, through their faith and through the power of the priesthood, literally control the elements.

Elder L. Tom Perry, Elder Robert L. Simpson, and I, accompanied by our wives, were assigned to hold a great regional conference in Tonga. The meeting was attended by thousands and thousands of Church members. Our conference was to be held in the open soccer stadium of the Liahona High School. No building on the island could hold such a large gathering.

It rained intermittently prior to the meeting, and I said to the local Tongan brethren, "What are the Saints going to do if it rains during the meeting?"

Their answer was, without any hesitation, "It is not going to rain."

I responded, "I certainly hope that is true. But what will we do if it rains?"

The brethren said, "Elder Faust, it will not rain." And it did not rain until our meeting was over. I have seen this same kind of faith many times.

35

THE NEED FOR NEW BEGINNINGS

If we do not promptly remove the slivers of sin and the thorns of carnal temptation, how can the Lord ever heal our souls?

I have learned from a lifetime making my living in an arena where I was not shadowboxing with life's problems that life is fuller and richer and better for those who are not afraid to make a new beginning.

Some time ago I attended a stake conference where the stake president, in our private meeting before the other meetings of the conference began, wanted to discuss a problem concerning one of his high councilors. Some ten years before, this high councilor had been involved in a grave sin, the penalty for which is excommunication. The high councilor had never made a confession. Short of making a confession and being willing to accept the punishment that would follow, however, the high councilor had done all in his power to rectify the matter and live so as to enjoy the blessings of the Church. The stake president did not learn of the transgression from the high councilor or his wife, but learned about it from a collateral source who swore the stake president to secrecy. The stake president was obliged to respect the confidence.

In a public meeting where the high councilor was present, the stake president spoke concerning repentance. He was directing his remarks to the high councilor, pleading and urging that he come forward voluntarily, make a confession, and begin the road to repentance.

My heart ached for the high councilor because had he come forward when the incident first occurred, by now it would have been possible for him to have the whole matter put at rest. He could have had a new beginning. Without his confession and willingness to accept the punishment, there could be no new beginning. Surely, repentance is one of the great principles of the gospel. No one is perfect, and we all have need to invoke this principle. For those who have been involved in serious transgressions, however, it is a life-saving principle. The longer we go down the wrong road, the harder it is to come back and get on the right road.

36

A Meeting by a Well

You cannot convert people beyond your own conversion.

My great-grandfather Henry Jacob Faust was born in a small village called Heddesheim in Rheinland, Prussia. The family went to the United States, and Grandfather Faust went through Salt Lake City on his way west to find his fortune in the gold fields of California. As he was going down through Utah, he stopped at a well in a little town called Fillmore. There he met a young lady named Elsie Ann Akerley. Grandfather was not a member of our Church. This young girl he met was a member. She had crossed the plains with the pioneers. Soon they fell in love. Grandfather went to California and stayed only long enough to get enough gold for a wedding band and then came back to Fillmore, where they were married.

Grandfather was not converted to the Church by the missionaries. I believe he was converted in the main by the testimony of this young girl he met by the well in Fillmore. Grandfather was later appointed by Brigham Young to be the first bishop of Corinne, Utah. At that time Grandfather was helping bring the railroad to Utah. I am grateful to my grandmother Elsie Ann Akerley, who as a young girl bore her testimony to this strange young man, Henry Jacob Faust from Germany, and helped convert him to the Church.

37

THE TRUE MARKS OF BEAUTY

*Women should follow the noble, intuitive feelings
planted deep within their souls by Deity in the previ-
ous world.*

Greatness and femininity have precious little to do with fine figures and physical beauty. They are something far greater. For many years, our family was friends with a little woman by the name of Ella Hoover. We knew her for over fifty years. When she was a babe, her father took her in his arms, like all of us fathers have done, and lovingly and playfully threw her into the air. When she came down, somehow, to his great sorrow, she slipped and fell to the floor and injured her back. She grew up to be a cripple and a dwarf, about thirty-six inches tall. The only normal things about Ella were her head and her great spirit and her tremendous charm. She grew up not feeling sorry for herself. She was always in pain, walking with a crutch in those days, later confined to a wheelchair.

Ella decided to learn to play the piano, despite her little stubby fingers. When you watched her play you almost didn't want to look, because it was not graceful. She decided that she wanted to learn to take care of herself. So she learned to type. Then she went to BYU, where she won the love of and was married in the temple to a full-sized, six-foot-tall man by the name of Bill Hoover. After a time, through a miracle as great as any miracle ever was, she conceived and carried and was delivered of a normal, full-sized man child. Of course, they named him Billy. And Ella's cup ran over.

One Sunday afternoon, after visiting their family in Magna, she and Bill and Billy were driving east on Thirty-third South in Salt Lake City and had a flat tire. Bill got out to see which of the tires was flat, and somebody from behind, drunk with wine, came along and hit Bill and killed him right in front of Ella's eyes. Bill was buried, leaving Ella with that little boy to take care of.

To make a long story short, Billy grew up and went on a mission, got married in the temple, and had grandchildren to bless Ella's life. Wherever Ella went, she was the center of attention. She was always chuckling and laughing and smiling, and people gravitated to her. At first they didn't want to look as she walked and moved, but they would become so intrigued with her great charm and great femininity that they would get close to her. She never felt sorry for herself over the eighty-some years of her life.

I am reminded as I recount the life of little Ella how little—how precious little—greatness has to do with fine figures and physical beauty, because femininity as a part of divinity is much, much more.

38

WHAT WORDS CANNOT CONVEY

Missionary work is a natural manifestation of the
pure love of Christ.

In World War II, I was stationed at an army camp in
Pennsylvania. We lived in a little ward in which our stake
patriarch also lived. His name was William G. Stoops.
Brother Stoops worked at a machine shop in the little town
of Waynesboro, Pennsylvania. Everyone called him Pappy.
He was a kindly, gentle, wonderful exemplary member of the
Church. All who met him honored and admired him. One
time a nonmember with whom he worked said something
like this: "I don't know much about the Mormon Church. I
have never met with the missionaries, and I have never studied the doctrine. I have never been to one of their services,

but I know Pappy Stoops and if the Church produces men like Pappy Stoops, it has to have much good in it."

We never know the power of our own example for either good or bad.

39

FOLLOW THE BRETHREN

If you take each challenge one step at a time, with faith in every footstep, your strength and understanding will increase. You cannot foresee all of the turns and twists ahead.

As I finished my first mission in Brazil, World War II was raging. We were told that Hitler planned to conquer the United States by coming up through South America. In an effort to stop what was called the Nazi Fifth Column activity, the United States government, through the state department, was recruiting Americans who knew the language, country, and culture. They would perform diplomatic work, including intelligence gathering.

Some of us who were completing our missions were offered positions in the state department, and some were named as vice-consuls of the United States. We were offered pay at a rate of about twenty times what our parents were sending us, and fifteen times what draftees in the armed forces of the United States were paid. Those who accepted this invitation could live out the war safely and comfortably without eating Spam or K-rations; they would not be shot at and would have plenty of money to spend.

One of my companions who was offered such a position asked his parents about the advisability of accepting such employment. My companion's father went to see President J. Reuben Clark Jr. The counsel received from the First Presidency was that we all should come home and be subject to the draft. We were encouraged not to put ourselves in a position of compromising our standards, nor to do anything inconsistent with our callings and priesthood. We were too young, inexperienced, and immature to understand fully what President Clark already knew.

Most of the missionaries accepted the counsel of President Clark and came home. A few did not, but they also made a contribution to the United States. In my immature mind, I could rationalize that there was more than one way to fight a war. Was it not justifiable to do anything, literally anything, to thwart the efforts of the hated Nazis? Were we not justified in doing anything and everything to defeat this evil empire that was seeking world domination? I questioned which was more honorable: to be drafted into the armed forces, where I might have to shoot someone and be shot at, or be in civilian life and fight the Nazis in a more subtle form of opposition.

I have subsequently learned that those who are innocently required to defend their country in combat will be excused from the consequences, but when we choose to be involved in other actions, we might not be. I have been grateful that, having followed the counsel of President Clark, we were not required to compromise our standards. Two of my companions who followed the same counsel later became General Authorities of the Church.

40

THE NEED TO RECEIVE

I hope none of our people will be too proud to accept help when they are in need.

My father was a successful lawyer, but not many years after the Depression he had two sons on a mission at the same time—my older brother, Gus, and me. Father fell ill and was hospitalized, and financially things became difficult. Our good bishop went to him and said, "George, this month the ward is going to send the money to your two missionary sons while you get back on your feet."

I did not learn of this until some years later, but I was grateful that my father, who gave generously to the Church all of his life, was not too proud in a moment of need to accept the help of the loving brothers and sisters in the ward. After all, that is the spirit of the gospel. In order to have the blessing of giving, one needs to receive.

41

FROM SMALL SEEDS

What can justify the great expenditure of effort, time, and means to "go . . . into all the world" (Mark 16:15), as the Savior commanded? The answer is simple. We can offer the hope promised by the Savior.

Some years ago, I received a letter from Luiz Valeixo, of Curitiba, Parana, Brazil. The letter was dated near the end of February 1990, and he wrote to remind me that it had been fifty years from the date of February 10 that Elder William Grant Bangerter and I first contacted his home. It was my first day tracting in Curitiba, and I could speak no Portuguese. We started up the street, and Elder Bangerter, my senior, took all of the houses for a block or so. Then he turned to me and said, "This is your house."

Fear struck in my heart. Since there were no doorbells, I clapped my hands together beyond the fence to get the attention of someone in the residence. Usually the maid responded. An older gray-haired lady leaned out of the window and asked in Portuguese, "What do you want?" I was in complete agony. I turned to my companion for help, but he kept his head down, marking in the tracting book. The passing seconds seemed like ages. In my heart, I prayed that I would be delivered. Just about then, she said, "Would you like to come in?" My feelings changed from agony to ecstasy.

In time, my companion and I moved on; others did most of the teaching and baptized the grandmother, the daughter, and all of her children. This was the first family to join the Church in Curitiba. There are now numerous stakes there.

Many years after that first meeting, Elder Charles Didier and I, with our wives, went to a regional conference in Curitiba. Most, if not all, of the remaining members of the Valeixo family came to the airport. It had been forty-five years since I first went to their door. Only the grandchildren of the original family are left, and now they have grown old. I did not recognize any of them. One by one, they came up to introduce themselves and fell upon me with *abraços* and tears. One of the granddaughters, now an old lady, held my hands and bathed them with her tears. As the tears wet the back of my hands, she rubbed them into the skin as though they were salve.

My companion and I were only the messengers. There was nothing about us that was important except our message. But the members of this family have had the conviction now for fifty years that my companion and I had brought them the message of joy and of eternal life.

42

REWARDS FOR AN "HONEST GUY"

We all need to know what it means to be honest.
Honesty is more than not lying.

Recently a local television channel ran the story of a ten-year-old boy named Josh Bowers from West Jordan, Utah. He found a wallet that had $530 in it. Josh didn't hesitate. He picked it up and took it to his mother. The wallet belonged to a mother of four, and the $530 was rent money she couldn't live without.

Josh had some compelling reasons to keep the money. His father had recently been disabled on the job, so his family was living on Social Security. Then there were all the things Josh could have bought with the money. What he really wanted, as he said, was a new bike. But he knew the money was not his and that someone needed that money. The relieved young mother gave Josh $40 for returning the wallet and the money.

Josh planned to use some of the money to get his old bike tire fixed. But a viewer, on hearing the story, had Josh pick out a brand-new bike "to reward him for being an honest guy." Interestingly, the donor of the bike wanted to remain anonymous, but he said, "Josh set an example that everybody should follow, and he looks happy" ("Honest Boy Returns Lost Wallet and Money," KUTV News, Salt Lake City, Utah, 8 and 10 September 1998, 10:00 P.M.).

We may not all get a shiny new bicycle as a reward for our honesty, but a feeling of goodness will shine within us for doing what we know is honest and true. Ultimately, we will receive an eternal reward.

43

POWER FROM THE SABBATH

Who can question but that sincere Sabbath obser-
vance will help keep [us] unspotted from the world?
The injunction to keep the Sabbath day holy is a con-
tinuing covenant between God and his elect.

I confess that as a young boy, Sunday was not my favorite day. Grandfather shut down the action. We didn't have any transportation. We couldn't drive the car. He wouldn't even let us start the motor. We couldn't ride the horses, or the steers, or the sheep. It was the Sabbath, and by commandment, the animals also needed rest. We walked to Church and everywhere else we wanted to go. I can honestly say that we observed both the spirit and the letter of Sabbath worship.

By today's standards, perhaps Grandfather's interpretation

of Sabbath day activities seems extreme, but something wonderful has been lost in our lives. To this day, I have been pondering to try to understand fully what has slipped away. Part of it was knowing that I was well on the Lord's side of the line. Another part was the feeling that Satan's influence was farther away. Mostly it was the reinforcement received by the spiritual power that was generated. We had the rich feeling that the spiritual "fulness of the earth" (D&C 59:16) was ours, as promised by the Lord.

44

WHAT IS WITHIN

If we could recognize the true greatness of women,
we would not treat them as we sometimes do.

Some years ago I sat as a spectator in a heartrending courtroom drama concerning the custody of some children. The contention was that the natural mother was not a good housekeeper, which was intended to add fuel to the claim that she was an unfit mother. A caseworker had testified that when she visited the family home it was in a shambles and that the kitchen was dirty.

The natural mother seeking to keep custody of her children was called to the stand. A middle-aged, somewhat unattractive lady came forward, took the oath, and sat in the witness stand. The attorney for the father, who had remarried and wanted the custody of the children, followed up relentlessly on the testimony already provided by the caseworker. His questions to the beleaguered mother were penetrating.

"Isn't it a fact," he asked, "that your house was as dirty as a pigpen the day the caseworker came?" What drama! How could the mother answer in her own best interest and protect her custody of the children? What should she say? There was electricity in the air!

She hesitated for a tense moment, and then she responded, calmly, with complete self-assurance: "Yes, my house certainly was a mess that day."

Her honesty obviously surprised even the judge, for he leaned over the bench and asked, "What do you mean, 'that day'?"

"Well, your honor," she replied, "earlier that morning when the caseworker came I had been bottling peaches. I had peeled, cooked, and bottled two bushels of peaches. I had not finished cleaning up the mess when the caseworker came. My sink was still sticky from the syrup that had spilled over when I tried to pour it into the bottles before they were sealed. My house certainly was a mess that day. I try to be a good house-keeper, but with three children I can't possibly keep it straight all the time."

Her frankness and candor were absolutely disarming and devastating to the opposition. When she finished, everyone in the courtroom knew the judge would rule in her favor. As she arose and stepped down from the witness stand, she had the bearing and self-assurance of a queen.

45

THE RACE IS NOT TO THE SWIFT

In my experience there are very few people who are of true genius. There are many who are gifted, but most of the world's work and great things come from ordinary people with a talent which they develop.

The most gifted athlete at our university excelled at every sport. He played football and ran the hurdles—in fact, he held the conference record in the low hurdles. Our coach, Ike Armstrong, required that the sprinters run once a week with the quarter-milers for 300 yards to increase the stamina of the sprinters and increase the speed of the quarter-milers. My friend—the great athlete—would lead all of the runners for about 275 yards, but as soon as the first quarter-miler passed him he would quit and wouldn't even finish. His natural talent and ability was such that he never had to extend himself to excel. He married, but the marriage failed. He went on into professional football and was something of a star until he got into the drug scene and died from the debilitating effects of drugs and alcohol. Others with much less talent have achieved far more.

Like the old fable of the tortoise and the rabbit, the plodders who make a contribution every day are the ones who, after years of labor, are able to achieve. The workhorses, not the show horses, seem to get the work done in the end.

46

OUR LEADER AND OUR FRIEND

Those who are called to lead in the ministry of the
Master are called to be good shepherds.

From the time I can remember being conscious of stake leaders, I knew what a stake president should be. Before being called as a General Authority, President Henry D. Moyle was president of the Cottonwood Stake and lived in our ward. He was our leader. He was our example. We knew we could achieve anything because President Moyle was guiding us. As we grew older, every time we applied for a job or to enter a school, we would always put down, as a reference, the name of our stake president. We knew of his personal interest in us. We knew he would help us if he could.

I have tried to analyze why President Moyle had such a

profound influence in our lives. I think it was because of his personal interest in us. He was our friend. We knew that he was always there when we needed him. It was said of him that when Henry Moyle loved you, he loved you through and through.

47

RICH IN THE THINGS THAT MATTER

*The Lord can do remarkable things with a person of
ordinary ability who is humble, faithful, and diligent
in serving the Lord.*

One day, while serving as a missionary in São Paulo,
Brazil, my companion and I went out to visit a poor
sister who was widowed.

We arrived at a humble home in a very isolated area.
This home had a dirt floor and open windows without any
glass. The wind and the flies could come right through.
Never before in my life had I been in a home where people
live with open windows and a dirt floor. Despite this, the
house was clean and neat, curtains were hung, and the boards
on the inside of the house were whitewashed.

Despite being primitive, the home had a cozy feeling

about it. We asked after this poor widow's health and well-being. She seemed quite happy and contented. We then began to have something of a gospel lesson. She participated freely. We thought that we were the teachers, but it soon became apparent that she knew more than we did. Her faith was deep, and her knowledge of the great eternal truths of where we came from, who we are, and where we are going was very profound.

I had my eyes opened. It was astonishing to hear this sister in these humble circumstances explain the great purposes of God in the grand scheme of the earth and its creation. I was reminded about what James said in his great epistle: "Hath not God chosen the poor of this world rich in faith, and heirs of the kingdom which he hath promised to them that love him?" (James 2:5).

This poor widow on the outskirts of São Paulo made the most of her straitened circumstances—circumstances that could not easily be changed. She realized that she should not make her life miserable by wishing it were otherwise. This impoverished woman enjoyed her independence, and she owed no one any money. She was industrious and thrifty. She crocheted beautiful cloths which were sold in the city to satisfy her simple wants, but she was not poor in spirit. She was rich in the things that really matter.

48

ANCHORING OUR STAKES

*Our stakes must be anchored deep in spiritual soil. If
they are not well secured, the wind of Satan's wrath
will loosen the fabric among the people of the Church
we are called upon to secure and hold spiritually tight.*

When I was a boy, my Uncle Jim took my brothers and me to see the Greatest Show on Earth, the Ringling Brothers Circus. I remember the small city of tents erected to house and protect the circus people, animals, and property. We came early enough to see them raise the huge tent where the people sat to see the performances. As the canvas was being erected, large iron stakes were pounded into the ground by strong men, each holding a sledge hammer. They stood in a circle around each stake, swinging their hammers in turn. They would sing in cadence to give them a rhythm as they took turns pounding the stakes deep into the ground. Elephants were used to pull the canvas over the high poles. When their work was finished, the whole huge tent was firm and taut. It was able to stand firm in the strongest storm.

We have all seen tents blown over by the wind and storm because the stakes were not sufficiently well-anchored. Figuratively, then, the whole Church can be likened unto a great tent held in place by its stakes firmly anchored as "a refuge from the storm, and from wrath when it shall be poured out without mixture upon the whole earth" (D&C 115:6).

49

BROADENING OUR VISION

Satan has had great success with this gullible genera-
tion. There is, however, an ample shield against the
power of Lucifer and his hosts.

Some years ago I was in Venice, Italy, to attend the conference of that stake. As we made our way to the stake
center where some of the meetings were to be held, we
faced heavy traffic going both ways. All of a sudden, I noticed
the strangest looking motorcycle coming towards us. It had a
normal-sized plastic windshield, which covered the front of
the motorcycle to protect the rider, but almost the whole
windshield was painted over. The rider could not see through
it except for a little clear space at eye level about six inches
by eight inches square. I could not understand why the rider

of that motorcycle had so limited his vision of where he was going and the dangers around him.

The priesthood of God is a shield. It is a shield against the evils of the world. That shield needs to be kept clean; otherwise, our vision of our purpose and the dangers around us will be limited. The cleansing agent is personal righteousness, but not all will pay the price to keep their shields clean. The Lord said, "For many are called, but few are chosen" (Matthew 22:14). We are called when hands are laid upon our heads and we are given the priesthood, but we are not chosen until we demonstrate to God our righteousness, our faithfulness, and our commitment.

50

AN UNBROKEN CHAIN

*We do cherish our temple buildings, but the buildings
alone do not bless.*

Some years ago, Sister Faust and I visited the Kirtland Temple. Our visit there happened on the evening of a perfect day in autumn. We were very inspired by the quiet location, the magnificent architecture, and the majesty of the special qualities of the building, the design of which was given by the Lord. We were impressed by everything about the building. Professor T. E. McDonald, architectural historian at the University of Illinois, describes the Kirtland Temple as follows: "Although there are in the world many temples, cathedrals, and churches of architectural and historical interest, yet of all these there is none more unique architecturally and more interesting historically than the temple which these Latter-day Saints built in the little village of Kirtland."

When I went back to Salt Lake after that visit to the Kirtland Temple, I was still under strong feelings and impressions about the building. I expressed to my brethren sadness that we do not have possession of that historic edifice.

I said to President Spencer W. Kimball, "President, we just need to have that building."

He replied, "Why don't you get it for us."

Elder Boyd K. Packer, however, remarked by way of comfort that, while we do not have the building, which of course is a great loss, we have what is not only important, but necessary. We still have in our custody and charge all of the keys and saving principles and ordinances to be administered in the other active temples, which keys, principles, and ordinances are intact and secure and will operate in all temples. These keys, principles, and ordinances, however, are not physical in nature—they are sacred gifts held by our loving prophet, to be used and delegated as he deems necessary for carrying on the work.

We also do not have the original Nauvoo Temple. But I and many others are inheritors of the blessings of the ordinances and covenants given in that building. I have in my possession the registry of the Nauvoo Temple that records when one of my great-grandfathers, John Akerley, received his endowments. That was the time when the Saints were preparing for the great exodus. Brigham Young's diary notes that he set a date for the closing of the temple so they could begin the march. When he went by the temple, he saw the Saints in long lines and his heart softened. He then decided, I am sure in council with his brethren of the Twelve, to operate the temple night and day until everyone who wished to do so had an opportunity to go through. There were not enough garments, and the brethren and sisters had to trade off garments to receive their endowments.

It was a special blessing that President Young felt to do that, because John Akerley, and others also endowed in Nauvoo, perished on the way to the West. His bones lie in Cutler's Park in the Winter Quarters area. Had he not been privileged to receive his endowments in this life, his descendants would have had a broken chain. The Nauvoo Temple built by the early Saints is long gone, but the blessings and covenants received by John and Jane Akerley continue to bless their descendants.

51

THE DEVIL'S THROAT

It is not good practice to become intrigued by Satan and his mysteries. No good can come from getting close to evil.

In the world there are many things of value to discover and much more to live for and hope for; however, as you move forward, you should be careful not to get too close to the Devil's Throat.

As a young man I served a mission to Brazil. It was a marvelous experience. I have returned many times since then in my Church assignments. One of the wonders of the world in that great country is Iguaçu Falls. In the flood season, the volume of water spilling over the brink is the largest in the world. Every few minutes, millions of gallons of water cascade into the chasm below. One part of the falls, where the deluge is the heaviest, is called the Devil's Throat. Large rocks are situated in the area just before the water rushes down into the Devil's Throat.

Some of the braver Brazilians used to take passengers in canoes to stand on those rocks and look down into the Devil's Throat. The water above the falls is usually calm and slow-moving and the atmosphere tranquil. Except for the roar of the water below, there is no way to anticipate the danger that is just a few feet beyond. A sudden, unexpected current could take a canoe into the rushing waters, over the cliff, and down into the Devil's Throat. While standing on a rock, a loss of footing or vertigo would have the same effect.

Spiritually, a Devil's Throat is concealed beneath the deceptively calm tranquility of our lives and the world in which we live. Each of us has to have the strength and integrity not to get too close to the Devil's Throat. Bravado in the face of certain death, physical or spiritual, is foolhardy.

Sometimes our youth will challenge things, such as parents' authority, society, values, religion. When I was a lawyer, I had a client who was a very successful contractor. But he challenged things. For instance, he argued that the earth is flat. I really think he knew it is round, but he would challenge it. By that time in my life, I had traveled around the world. In World War II, I was assigned over a period of time to go west from San Francisco to Cairo and West Africa, and later to Brazil, and then home. But I knew the earth was round before I circled the globe.

You will do well not to challenge some things in life. This is particularly so with the commandments of God. I am very grateful for the principle of repentance, for we all make mistakes. But it is far better to make the right choice in the first place.

52

LEARNING TO WANT
THE GIFTS YOU GET

*This Christmas, as I have done for many years, I will
remember my parents with gratitude and love.
Among other things, I will remember them for the
Christmas ring they gave me as a child, which I did
not then fully appreciate.*

I am told that "there are generally two kinds of Christmas
gifts: the ones you don't like and the ones you don't get"
(*20,000 Quips and Quotes*, comp. Evan Esar, 1995, 135).
However, as someone once said, "Some luck lies in *not getting*
what you thought you *wanted* but getting what you *have*,
which once you have got it you may be smart enough to see is
what you *would have wanted* had you *known*" (Garrison

Keillor, in *The Third and Possibly the Best 637 Best Things Anybody Ever Said,* comp. Robert Byrne, 1988, 378).

When I was a small boy, I was very anxious about what Santa Claus was going to bring me for Christmas. I was fascinated by mechanical toys—in fact, I even invented a few. One of my favorite aunts accused me of having wheels in my head.

For one of my inventions, I would loop a string around the spindle of the milk separator and then to a spool on a nail some distance away. By turning the handle on the separator, the rotating spindle would cause the string belt to turn the spool on the nail. I would then loop another string from the first spool to a second spool and even to a third. If you cranked the separator very fast, the spools would really spin. It was great fun. I thought it was an engineering masterpiece.

Because of this interest in mechanical toys, I had a great interest in owning a toy called Sandy Andy. A Sandy Andy had a small bucket that, pulled by a counterweight, would travel up a track to a sand-loaded bin. At the top of the track the bucket would load up with sand; then by force of gravity it would go back down the track and empty the sand into another container. It would then come back up the track for a refill. If you replenished the sand in the upper container, it would work all day. Long before Christmas, I made it perfectly clear to all concerned that I would like a Sandy Andy for Christmas.

A few weeks before Christmas, my older brother came down to my bedroom with a ring sizer, which he tried on my fingers. I paid no attention to what he was doing. It never occurred to me that I would get a ring for Christmas instead of the Sandy Andy. Christmas morning came, and I was greatly disappointed to find that my parents had given me a ring. It had no precious stone, but was beautiful in its simplicity. It had been made especially for me, but it was certainly not what I wanted.

I am afraid my disappointment was so obvious that my parents sat me down and asked me what was wrong. I told them that I had not received the Sandy Andy that I wanted so much. They relented, and a few days later I received a Sandy Andy. I literally wore out the Sandy Andy in about three weeks. But I had little interest in the ring, and it was soon forgotten and misplaced. I have never found the ring. In my childish feelings I did not realize that my parents gave me the ring as a lasting expression of their love for me.

As I grew older and my feelings for my parents matured, I began to regret my actions. Now, with both my parents gone, I wish I had that specially made ring, which my parents had given to me as a token of their love. If I had it now, it would be a treasured heirloom that I would like to pass on to one of my grandsons.

53

TO RUN AND NOT BE WEARY

When I was a boy, one frequently maligned doctrine was the Word of Wisdom. Some took offense when Church leaders taught it.

When I was the president of the Cottonwood Stake, one of our stake patriarchs was Dr. Creed Haymond. He would occasionally bear strong testimony of the Word of Wisdom. As a young man he was the captain of the University of Pennsylvania track team. In 1919 Brother Haymond and his team were invited to participate in the annual Inter-Collegiate Association track meet. The night before the track meet, his coach, Lawson Robertson, who coached several Olympic teams, instructed his team members to drink some sherry wine. In those days, coaches wrongly felt that wine was a tonic for muscles hardened through rigorous training. All the other team members took the sherry, but Brother Haymond refused because his parents had taught him the Word of Wisdom. Brother Haymond became very anxious because he did not like to be disobedient to his coach. He was to compete against the fastest men in the world. What if he made a poor showing the next day? How could he face his coach?

The next day at the track meet the rest of the team members were very ill and performed poorly or were even too sick to run. Brother Haymond, however, felt well and won the 100- and 220-yard dashes. His coach told him, "You just ran the two hundred and twenty yards in the fastest time it has ever been run by any human being." That night and for the rest of his life, Creed Haymond was grateful for his simple faith in keeping the Word of Wisdom.

54

FAITH, COURAGE, AND PERSEVERANCE

One of humankind's greatest blessings is for righteous
womanhood to be "the perfect workmanship of God."

L et me tell you of one young woman who has demonstrated remarkable strength in the face of great tragedy. On April 17, 1999, a big van broadsided a car and severely injured sixteen-year-old Emily Jensen. Her skull was fractured, and she was in a coma for three months, and six months in the hospital. She has had to learn everything again as if from birth. It would have been easy to give up, but giving up is not in Emily's vocabulary. She works so hard at recovery that she runs the equivalent of a twenty-six-mile marathon every day. Her faith, courage, and perseverance have strengthened and motivated many other hospital patients.

Emily is still working very hard to regain her speech. Even so, she fearlessly asks nurses, technicians, and therapists, "Are you a Mormon?" If they reply no, she tells them in her muddled sentences, "You should be. Read the Book of Mormon." Emily dictated to her mother what she wanted written in five copies of the Book of Mormon that she gave to a doctor, three therapists, and a technician before she left the hospital.

Emily dearly loved one technician who had become totally inactive in the Church. They prayed together in Emily's hospital room. In language that was difficult to understand, but with a spirit that was strong and clear, Emily told her that she needed to go back to church. That technician later wrote Emily: "I want to thank you so much for the Book of Mormon you gave me. I cried when I read what you wrote. I know someday I will love this book as much as you do."

Emily's life was recently brightened at Skyline High School in Salt Lake City. The student body picked her as this year's prom queen in recognition of her extraordinary courage. Her classmates stood and cheered as she struggled to the stage of the packed auditorium, supported on the arm of the student body president. Though she continues to go each day for therapy, Emily's life is still defined by her spiritual identity, her goodness, her kindness to others, and her strong testimony.

55

TRUSTING IN GOD'S PROMISES

Hope is the anchor of our souls. I know of no one
who is not in need of hope—young or old, strong or
weak, rich or poor.

Not long ago, I visited Elder Orin Voorheis at his parents' home in Pleasant Grove, Utah. He is a big, handsome, splendid young man who served in the Argentina Buenos Aires South Mission. One night, about eleven months into his mission, some armed robbers accosted Elder Voorheis and his companion. In a senseless act of violence, one of them shot Elder Voorheis in the head. For days he hovered between life and death, unable to speak, hear, move, or even breathe on his own. Through the faith and prayers of a host of people over a long period of time, he eventually was taken off life support and brought back to the United States.

After months of extensive hospitalization and therapy, Elder Voorheis became stronger, but he was still paralyzed and unable to speak. Progress was slow. His parents decided that they should bring their son home and care for him in the loving atmosphere of their own family. However, their modest home lacked the space or equipment to give the needed therapy. Many kind neighbors, friends, and benefactors pitched in to build an addition to the home and provide physical therapy equipment.

Elder Voorheis is still almost completely paralyzed and unable to speak, but he has a wonderful spirit and can respond to questions with hand movements. He still wears his missionary badge. His parents do not ask, "Why did this happen to our noble son, who was serving at the call of the Master?" No one has a certain answer except perhaps in circumstances where higher purposes are served. We must walk in faith. We recall the Savior's reply to the question, "Who did sin, this man, or his parents, that he was born blind?" The Savior answered that no one was at fault but that the works of God might be manifest in him (see John 9:1–3). Rather than harbor bitterness, the members of the Voorheis family bow their heads and say to the Lord: "Thy will be done. We have been grateful for him every day of his life, and with the help of others we will willingly bear the burden of caring for him."

My purpose in visiting Elder Voorheis was to join his father, his bishop, his home teacher, and others in giving him a blessing of hope. Some may ask, "Is there hope for Elder Voorheis in this life?" I believe there is great hope for everyone! Sometimes we ask God for miracles, and they often happen, but not always in the manner we expect. The quality of Elder Voorheis's life is less than desirable, but the influence of his life on others is incalculable and everlasting both here and in Argentina. Indeed, after his accident the Kilómetro 26 Branch, where he served in Argentina, grew rapidly and quickly qualified for the construction of a chapel.

Hope is trust in God's promises, faith that if we act now, the desired blessings will be fulfilled in the future. Abraham "against hope believed in hope, that he might become the father of many nations." Contrary to human reason, he trusted God, "fully persuaded" that God would fulfill His promises of giving Abraham and Sarah a child in their old ages (see Romans 4:18–21).

56

A LESSON FROM A LAMB

The bearers of the priesthood have a great responsibility, whether they be fathers, grandfathers, home teachers, elders quorum presidents, bishops, stake presidents, or hold other Church callings.

When I was a very small boy, my father found a lamb all alone out in the desert. The herd of sheep to which its mother belonged had moved on, and somehow the lamb got separated from its mother, and the shepherd must not have known that it was lost. Because it could not survive alone in the desert, my father picked it up and brought it home. To have left the lamb there would have meant certain death, either by falling prey to the coyotes or by starvation because it was so young that it still needed milk. Some sheepmen call these lambs "bummers." My father gave the lamb to me, and I became its shepherd.

For several weeks I warmed cow's milk in a baby's bottle and fed the lamb. We became fast friends. I called him Nigh—why, I don't remember. It began to grow. My lamb and I would play on the lawn. Sometimes we would lie together on the grass and I would lay my head on its soft, woolly side and look up at the blue sky and the white billowing clouds. I did not lock my lamb up during the day. It would not run away. It soon learned to eat grass. I could call my lamb from anywhere in the yard by just imitating as best I could the bleating sound of a sheep: *Baa. Baa.*

One night there came a terrible storm. I forgot to put my lamb in the barn that night as I should have done. I went to bed. My little friend was frightened in the storm, and I could hear it bleating. I knew that I should help my pet, but I wanted to stay safe, warm, and dry in my bed. I didn't get up as I should have done. The next morning I went out to find my lamb dead. A dog had also heard its bleating cry and killed it. My heart was broken. I had not been a good shepherd or steward of that which my father had entrusted to me. My father said, "Son, couldn't I trust you to take care of just one lamb?" My father's remark hurt me more than losing my woolly friend. I resolved that day, as a little boy, that I would try never again to neglect my stewardship as a shepherd if I were ever placed in that position again.

Not too many years thereafter I was called as a junior companion to a home teacher. There were times when it was so cold or stormy and I wanted to stay home and be comfortable, but in my mind's ear I could hear my little lamb bleating, and I knew I needed to be a good shepherd and go with my senior companion. In all those many years, whenever I have had a desire to shirk my duties, there would come to me a remembrance of how sorry I was that night so many years ago when I had not been a good shepherd. I have not always done everything I should have, but I have tried.

Even today, after more than sixty years, I can still hear in my mind the bleating, frightened cry of the lamb of my boyhood that I did not shepherd as I should have. I can also remember the loving rebuke of my father: "Son, couldn't I trust you to take care of just one lamb?" If we are not good shepherds, I wonder how we will feel in the eternities.

57

THE SUPREME BENEDICTION OF LIFE

My inevitable eternal journey, if I am so favored, will be wonderful with my Ruth by my side.

Not long after I was called as a member of the Twelve, I was asked to address the topic of marriage in a meeting of all the General Authorities. In giving me the assignment, Elder Boyd K. Packer asked a very penetrating question: "What would you be without Ruth?"

I could have answered immediately, "Not much," but he already knew that. Instead, I took him seriously and spent the next twenty-four hours thinking about what I would have been without the loving, sweet support and the discipline of Ruth Wright in my life.

It shocked me a little to even think about what life would be and would have been without her. I would have to answer honestly that without my wife I would have been pretty much of a failure. I do not claim to be an expert in marriage. I have only been married once, but thanks to my good wife it took. I do not claim to have a better marriage than anyone, but I do claim to be married to a great companion.

Without going into all the experiences in marriage that have caused me to appreciate my wife so much, I cannot help remembering during the twenty years that I was a bishop and stake president, coming home tired and weary, and Ruth would say, "Have you called So-and-so?" I would say "No." I was without strength to look up the telephone number and dial it, so she would silently take the phone, dial the number, and hand it to me.

When I was called as an Area Supervisor, I remember leaving her in the hospital immediately after a serious operation to go to South America and find a home for us to live in. I also remember when I left that home in São Paulo some time later to deal with a difficult and dangerous situation that she did not say, "Do you have to go?" or "When will you be back?" She did as she has done all these years and sent me out with a kiss and her blessing, and with a silent encouragement to not come home until my work was done.

Perhaps in such times of great stress we can become what we ought to be in terms of our relationships with our wives, but perhaps the eternal everyday causes some of us to be more casual than we ought to be.

I know the gospel is true, and I know that a substantial part of that gospel is how I treat Ruth on an hour-by-hour, day-by-day, ongoing basis. I believe that none of us who holds the priesthood have or can come into full possession of all our powers without an eternal companion. I suppose the ultimate judgment will come to us in terms of what kind of a person we have been, what kind of a husband we have been, what kind of a father we have been, and what kind of a family we have raised.

I don't love anybody like I love my wife. My mother has Father, my children have their companions, but Ruth is me. Our wives become part of us. They become like our own flesh, and, as Paul has counseled, we should love them as much. The simple truth is, it is not good for man to be alone. The greatest sustaining influence in my mature life has been the constant, supporting, unqualified, unreserved love I have felt from my wife. That sacred relationship with my wife has been the supreme benediction of my life. I just can't imagine what life would have been like without having had that blessing.

SOURCES

1. "A Critical Crossroad," from "Stand Up and Be Counted," *Ensign*, February 1982, 69–70

2. "The Best Stand of Hay," from "Opening the Windows of Heaven," *Ensign*, November 1998, 54.

3. "It May Not Seem to Hurt as Much," from "It May Not Seem to Hurt as Much if You Don't Cry," *Friend*, September 1974, 12–13.

4. "Delivering in Our Dealings," from "Integrity, the Mother of Many Virtues," *Ensign*, May 1982, 47–48.

5. "'Suffer the Little Children,'" from "Gratitude As a Saving Principle," *Ensign*, May 1990, 86–87.

6. "Our Debt of Gratitude," from "Gratitude As a Saving Principle," *Ensign*, May 1990, 87.

7. "Setting a Standard," from "Honesty—A Moral Compass," *Ensign*, November 1996, 42.

8. "Withstanding the Thorns of Life," from "Crown of Thorns, Crown of Glory," *Ensign*, May 1991, 68.

9. "The Good That Can Grow Out of Tragedy," from "Five Loaves and Two Fishes," *Ensign*, May 1994, 6–7.

10. "Nurturing a Simple Faith," from "An Untroubled Faith," *BYU Speeches*, 28 September 1986, 46.

11. "Bearing Our Responsibilities," from "These I Will Make My Leaders," *Ensign*, November 1980, 34–35.

12. "The Very Appearance of Evil," from James E. Bell, *In the Strength of the Lord: The Life and Teachings of James E. Faust* (Salt Lake City: Deseret Book, 1999), 65.

13. "A Lesson in Leadership," from "These I Will Make My Leaders," *Ensign*, November 1980, 35.

14. "Earning the Confidence of Others," from "These I Will Make My Leaders," *Ensign*, November 1980, 36.

15. "Making It Do, or Doing Without," from "The Blessings We Receive As We Meet the Challenge of Economic Stress," *Ensign*, November 1982, 88.

16. "An Earned Legacy," from "The Keystone of Our Religion," *Ensign*, November 1983, 9, 11.

17. "'What Can You Do?'" from "Unwanted Messages," *Ensign*, November 1986, 8.

18. "Standing on Holy Ground," from "A Priceless Heritage," *Ensign*, November 1992, 84.

19. "Will We Accept the Gift?" from "The Message: A Christmas with No Presents," *New Era*, December 1984, 7

20. "A Blessing from the Lord," from "Priesthood Blessings," *Ensign*, November 1995, 63–64.

21. "Finding the Signal Point," from "Personal Epiphanies," Single Adult Fireside, 7 January 1996; extract printed in Bell, *In the Strength of the Lord*, 342.

22. "Spiritual Taproots," from "Heirs to the Kingdom of God," *Ensign*, May 1995, 63.

23. "Poise under Pressure," from "The Way of an Eagle," address to BYU faculty, 23 August 1994.

24. "The Permanence of the Family," from "The Weightier Matters of the Law: Judgment, Mercy, and Faith," *Ensign,* November 1997, 54.

25. "The Weightier Matters," from "The Weightier Matters of the Law: Judgment, Mercy, and Faith," *Ensign,* November 1997, 59.

26. "Begin with Our Own," from Regional Representatives seminar, 5 April 1985; excerpt in Bell, *In the Strength of the Lord,* 372–73.

27. "What Is of Worth," from "Self-Esteem—A Great Human Need," *BYU Speeches,* 23 August 1983, 191–92.

28. "'On My Honor,'" from " 'We Seek After These Things,'" *Ensign,* May 1998, 44.

29. "A Spirit That Shone," from "Self-Esteem—A Great Human Need," *BYU Speeches,* 23 August 1983, 192.

30. "'A Fine Christian You Are,'" from Christmas message to Young Ambassadors, San Diego, California, 16 December 1981.

31. "A Christmas with No Presents," from "The Message: A Christmas with No Presents," *New Era,* December 1984, 4, 6.

32. "The Day the Bishop Sang," from "The Need for Balance in Our Lives," *Ensign,* March 2000, 4–5.

33. "Well-Chosen Dreams," from *To Reach Even unto You* (Salt Lake City: Deseret Book, 1980), 17.

34. "The Power of Prayer," from Priesthood Fireside, 6 May 1990.

35. "The Need for New Beginnings," from "Beginnings,"

University of Utah Fireside, 27 September 1983; excerpt in Bell, *In the Strength of the Lord*, 300–301.

36. "A Meeting by a Well," from "The Importance of Bearing Testimony," *Ensign*, March 1997, 2.

37. "The True Marks of Beauty," from *To Reach Even Unto You*, 5.

38. "What Words Cannot Convey," from "The Importance of Bearing Testimony," *Ensign*, March 1997, 2.

39. "Follow the Brethren," from "A Legacy of the New Testament," Church Educational System address, 12 August 1988; excerpt in Bell, *In the Strength of the Lord*, 61.

40. "The Need to Receive," from address at LDS welfare center dedication in Ogden, Utah, 21 November 1991; excerpt in Bell, *In the Strength of the Lord*, 454.

41. "From Small Seeds," from "The Law—A Key to Something Greater," address to Clark Law Society, 30 April 1990; excerpt in Bell, *In the Strength of the Lord*, 61.

42. "Rewards for an 'Honest Guy,'" from "We Believe in You!" *BYU Speeches*, 1 November 1998, 52.

43. "Power from the Sabbath," from "The Lord's Day," *Ensign*, November 1991, 33.

44. "What Is Within," from "Self-Esteem—A Great Human Need," *BYU Speeches*, 23 August 1983, 192–93.

45. "The Race Is Not to the Swift," from "Self-Esteem—A Great Human Need," *BYU Speeches*, 23 August 1983, 193.

46. "Our Leader and Our Friend," from "The Stake President As a Spiritual Leader," satellite presentation, 22 August 1993; excerpt in Bell, *In the Strength of the Lord*, 28.

47. "Rich in the Things That Matter," from "Simply Happy," *New Era*, July 1985, 4.

48. "Anchoring Our Stakes," from "The Stake President As a Spiritual Leader," satellite presentation, 22 August 1993.

49. "Broadening Our Vision," in Bell, *In the Strength of the Lord*, 394; edited version of "The Priesthood of God," priesthood fireside, 6 May 1990.

50. "An Unbroken Chain," from Temple Presidents' Seminar, August 1988.

51. "The Devil's Throat," from "We Believe in You!" BYU Speeches, 1 November 1998, 51–52.

52. "Learning to Want the Gifts You Get," from "The Christmas Ring," First Presidency's Christmas Devotional, 5 December 1999.

53. "To Run and Not Be Weary," from "The Enemy Within," *Ensign*, November 2000, 44–45.

54. "Faith, Courage, and Perseverance," from "Womanhood: The Highest Place of Honor," *Ensign*, May 2000, 97.

55. "Trusting in God's Promises," from "Hope, An Anchor of the Soul," *Ensign*, November 1999, 59–60.

56. "A Lesson from a Lamb," from "Responsibilities of Shepherds," *Ensign*, May 1995, 46.

57. "The Supreme Benediction of Life," from an address presented at Association of Mormon Counselors and Psychotherapists convention, 2 October 1980; edited version in "Brethren, Love Your Wives," *Ensign*, July 1981, 35.

INDEX

ABOUT THE AUTHOR

President James E. Faust, second counselor in the First Presidency of The Church of Jesus Christ of Latter-day Saints, has served as a General Authority since October 1972, when he was called as an Assistant to the Quorum of the Twelve. In 1978 he was sustained as an apostle. President Faust began serving as second counselor to President Gordon B. Hinckley on March 12, 1995, at the age of seventy-four.

President Faust served a mission in Brazil and was an officer in the U.S. Army Air Corps in World War II prior to completing his studies in law at the University of Utah. His professional and civic activities have included service as president of the Utah Bar Association, member of the Utah State Legislature, adviser to the *American Bar Journal*, and vice-chairman of the board and chairman of the executive committee of the *Deseret News*. He and his wife, the former Ruth Wright, are the parents of five children.

He is also the author of *Finding Light in a Dark World*, *The Greatest Gift*, *The Power of Peace*, *Reach Up for the Light*, and *To Reach Even unto You*. His biography, *In the Strength of the Lord: The Life and Teachings of James E. Faust*, written by James P. Bell, was published in 1999 by Deseret Book.